Secrets of a Healthy, Wealthy & Happy Life

(Learned from Himalayan yogis, ashram gurus and from experiences shared by famous personalities)

RAVI DABRAL

(Author is the winner of International Man of Excellence Award for Education, Corporate & Social Services, and holds over twenty-five academic and professional qualifications)

This book is dedicated to the

Farmers, *who feed the world;*

Armed forces, *which protect nations;*

Teachers, *who build the nations;*

Students, *who are hope of the nations;*

Senior citizens, *the gold mine of experiences, values,*

morals and sanskars in this University of Life.

Women, *the real source of love, care and emotions –*

the beautiful flower in the Garden of Life.

[Ten percent of net profit from the sale of this book will go

to the welfare fund created to prevent suicide among

farmers and army personnel].

TABLE OF CONTENTS

1

SOURCE OF INSPIRATION

I have heard and read a lot about many famous international personalities such as Steve Jobs (late owner of Apple) and Mark Zuckerberg (owner of Facebook). They went to Uttarakhand (known as *Devbhoomi*, the abode of deities and gods) to learn spirituality under the patronage of ashram gurus and yogis, and after that became very successful, renowned, and wealthy personalities.

I was embarrassed to know that foreigners understood the importance of the spiritual powers of gurus and yogis of Himalayas, but, despite being a native of Uttarakhand, I never understood their role and significance.

For around fifteen years I conducted extensive studies, research, exploration, and investigation, and interacted with many Himalayan yogis and ashram gurus. Finally I found the secrets to get spiritual peace and material wealth, and the way to inculcate virtues and values, and how to eradicate vices such as greed, lust, and addiction.

During my stay at ashrams both in Rishikesh and Haridwar in Uttarakhand, and up the hills of Himalayas in India, I interacted with some of the renowned international personalities and came to know about their real-life experiences. On the condition of anonymity, they agreed to share their enlightened experiences for the benefit of the global readers and citizens.

I believe in sharing knowledge, so, through a series of books, both nonfiction and fiction, I have decided to share the material and spiritual secrets with global readers to make them healthy, wealthy, and happy.

I feel that after learning from these enriching experiences, together, as a team, we can make this world a better, safer and more peaceful place to live in.

I seek your blessings, best wishes, and support during this journey of bringing material wealth and spiritual peace to the global readers and citizens.

2

"CHANGE THE WORLD BY CHANGING MYSELF"

During my stay at Ashram, in order to utilise my research and investigative skills, the ashram guruji gave me an interesting assignment to explore the possibility of making Uttarakhand the spiritual capital of the world. For this purpose, he suggested that I prepare a report that he was willing to forward to the United Nations Educational, Scientific and Cultural Organization (UNESCO) for its consideration.

To complete this assignment, I travelled extensively and visited many ashrams in Rishikesh,

Haridwar, and in the high hills of Himalayas. I interacted and interviewed many yogis, gurus, and Indian and foreign learners to know their perspectives, and recorded their suggestions. They conveyed that in today's materialistic world, where vices such as greed, lust, and addiction have destroyed both internal and external peace, there is a great need to inculcate values, virtues, and morals among global citizens. This is to make this world a better and more peaceful place to live in, and Uttarakhand as a spiritual capital of the world can play a vital role in this mission.

■ ■ ■

Once I submitted my report to guruji for his review and inputs, he suggested that I participate in the 'self-reform' course. In this course, people from all over the world having different backgrounds and religions come and learn about the purification of body and soul through yoga and meditation. Guruji said, with a smile on his face, "You can consider it part of white magic to reform the society, just the opposite of black magic to take revenge from enemies."

At the beginning of the course, Guruji gave all learners a piece of paper with the heading "Change the World by Changing Myself," the content of which was as follows:

The Sufi Bayazid says this about himself:

I was a revolutionary when I was young, and my prayer to God was:

"Lord, give me the energy to change the world."

As I approached middle age and realised that half my life had passed without my changing a single soul, I changed my prayer to:

"Lord, give me the grace to change all those who come in contact with me—just my family and friends; and I shall be content."

Now that I am an old man and my days are numbered, my prayer is:

"Lord, give me the grace to change myself."

If I had prayed for this right from the start, I would not have wasted my life.

■ ■ ■

Guruji said, "During this self-reform process, please follow the rule 'learn, unlearn and relearn' to gain and retain knowledge.

1. To learn and adopt virtuous qualities to live a peaceful and stress-free life.

2. To unlearn and reject vices such as hatred, jealousy, comparison, expectation, gossiping, greed, lust, and addiction, which are responsible for about 50 per cent of our problems and stress.

3. To relearn, adapt, and follow good habits and healthy lifestyles."

■ ■ ■

I asked guruji, "What are these concepts such as self-reform, self-change, self-control, self-criticism, self-enrichment, self-transformation, self-realisation, introspection and conscience management? Please guide us as to how to implement these to improve our personal and professional life."

Guruji replied,

1. "Firstly, for effective self-change, be your own true friend by knowing your Strengths, Weaknesses, Opportunities, and Threats (SWOT Analysis) through a regular **self-criticism** process.

2. Keep in mind that **change is the only permanent** and dynamic thing in life.

3. Please remember that **disciplined lifestyle**, determination, courage, and faith, are needed to undergo self-change.

4. **Blame games**, excuses, procrastination, negative attitude, false ego, arrogance, bad habits, and addictions restrict the self-change, so immediately throw out these vices from your life."

One of the ashram learners asked guruji, "We understand the importance of 'self-change' to live a better personal, professional, and peaceful life, but why is it so challenging to change the self?"

Guruji replied, "Let me explain this to you through a story. It is said that a frog adjusts itself so well to changes in water temperature that it won't jump out of a pot even when the water is nearly boiling. So it dies! Similarly, we have adjusted and addicted ourselves to the materialistic philosophy of '**eat, drink, and be merry**,' and our mind and body resist any change until we die."

3

MATERIALISM PHILOSOPHY "EAT, DRINK, AND BE MERRY"

Guruji asked learners, "Do you know about the materialism philosophies of two mythological sages Brihaspati (teacher of gods) and Charvaka (teacher of devils)?

We all said, "No."

Guruji said, "As per Hindu mythology, there were two sages—Brihaspati and Charvaka. Sage Brihaspati, the teacher of deities, is regarded as the traditional founder of the materialistic school of thought. Sage Brihaspati intentionally propagated materialism philosophy ("eat, drink, and be merry") among the devils, so that their whole life they would be busy in all this and finally be ruined on their own without giving any trouble to deities. Sage Charvaka, said to be one of the chief disciples of sage Brihaspati, was impressed with the materialism philosophy.

Charvaka promoted and spread materialism philosophy among devils. As is popularly known, it is easier to be addicted to vices than to virtues, so this philosophy spread very fast, like fire in the jungle, and even reached the ordinary people and became a way of their routine lifestyle. People who used to earlier worship nature or deities due to their supernatural powers and virtues soon became addicted to a lifestyle full of materialism, and forgot to worship gods and to take care of nature. This resulted into diminishing of values, virtues, and morals. They adopted vices and bad habits of devils as their lifestyle, which continues even today in the modern society. That is why there is excessive violence, greed, lust, and addiction in today's world.

Materialistic way of life is the way of enjoying the pleasures of the five senses, leading to bodily enjoyment. Thus, it ignores the sixth sense, common sense, intellect, and reasoning power for virtuous decision making to live a stress free peaceful life.

For materialists, bodily enjoyment is the final end of human existence. The mind is considered a product of only four elements: air, water, fire, and earth; it rejects the fifth element, ether, which is linked with the soul as it is not perceived but inferred. Everything that exists, including the mind, as per sage Charvaka, is due to a particular combination of these four elements—earth, water, fire, and air. It may be a chemical process in the form of wild thoughts and dreams in the mind that led human beings to the illusion that they are special persons on this earth and should have values and ethics; these are mere phantoms created by a diseased mind. Consciousness is regarded as a mere product of these four elements. It is produced when these four elements combine in a certain proportion; it is always found associated with the body and vanishes when the body disintegrates.

There is no other world in this universe. Death means actual liberation, without any possibility of rebirth or reincarnation. There is no heaven, no final liberation nor any soul in another world. Similarly, the concept of soul and God are rejected as per materialism philosophy.

As per materialism philosophy, religion is the means of livelihood of the priests, and is propagated by kings, rulers and modern politicians through propaganda since the inception of civilisation, to fool and rule the innocent common public.

Modern followers of materialism philosophy believe that as virtuous as spiritualism philosophy might be, it only feeds the soul; and we don't even know whether the soul exists or not. Also, this spiritualism philosophy won't earn you money to feed yourself or your family which can only be possible by following and adopting materialism philosophy.

Guruji further said, "We effortlessly blame the outside world for being corrupt, but due to our inclination towards monetary things actually we are corrupt. Being a materialistic person in life is not necessarily all bad, but first one must deserve, through skills and hard work, to reserve those material things rather than choosing corrupt practices as a shortcut."

■ ■ ■

To conclude, guruji told us that materialism philosophy propagates sensual pleasure as the purpose of life. It believes in "eat, drink, and be merry." It holds that once the body is converted to ashes, there is no hope of coming back again on this earth. This materialism philosophy provided a basis for present-day concepts of greed, lust, and addiction, which are a kind of vices within us and are the main causes of most of the crimes in this world.

Guruji said, "Contrary to materialism philosophy, spiritualism philosophy believes that we must have virtues, values, and morals to live a stress-free, peaceful, purposeful, contended, enlightened, and happy life. What is spiritualism philosophy and how it can make our life a pleasant experience is something you will understand step by step soon in your 'self-reform' course."

Guruji further said, "As you know, 'a healthy mind lives in a healthy body' and 'health is wealth,' so, to move forward, let us first understand the meaning of 'health,' as maintaining a healthy body is the first step towards self-reform or self-change."

4

BODY HEALTH

Guruji said, "The holistic definition of health as given by *ayurveda* and World Health Organization (WHO) is that "it is a combination of physical, mental, social, and spiritual well-being."

Physical health refers to balanced dietary habits, moderate food quantity, control over health parameters, good sleep, not having an addiction, and the like.

Mental health relates to self-control; the ability to accept criticism; understanding the perspectives of others; empathy; having a positive attitude; not being driven by lust, greed, and addiction; not being jealous; not having expectations from others; not having the habit of comparison with others; having the confidence to face challenges in life; and having the ability to resolve issues using intellect and reasoning power.

Social health means having healthy and good relations with family members, relatives, friends, neighbours, and colleagues; a sense of brotherhood, respecting all religions and perspectives of others; and having a social welfare approach.

Spiritual health implies living a life with "virtues"; awareness of self as a soul; knowing that the body is just a carrier of the soul; working towards purity of soul; serving mankind and having a caring nature.

We need to understand that food is the fuel, primarily for upkeep of internal organs and running the internal machinery of our body. Taste, which can lead to excessive eating and hence becomes the reason for more diseases, should be a second priority. To live a healthy life, we need many important ingredients in food like carbohydrates, fats, proteins, vitamins, minerals, and so on in moderate quantities, popularly known as a balanced diet. The calorie intake for each individual is different as per work profile. In a city lifestyle, the calorie requirement of a person is lesser as compared to the village lifestyle. Human beings waste much time discussing politics, economics, philosophy, religion, media, cinema, sports, and so on, but ironically pay less attention to the type of food or ingredients they need to consume to live a healthy life.

Unfortunately and coincidently, most modern people believe in *charvaka* materialism philosophy of **"eat, drink, and be merry."** This philosophy focuses on sensual and bodily pleasures.

As per spiritualism philosophy, the body is the medium through which our soul expresses itself and experiences the world around us by following virtuous, righteous and spiritual path. Once we understand the true meaning of spiritualism, it is easy to get rid of old die-hard bad habits.

Guruji said, "Let us talk about three important aspects of a person's life—body, mind, and money."

Body health: Nowadays, doctors are more like commission agents of hospitals and pharmaceutical companies. They prescribe you medicines that temporary improve your condition but don't cure you completely. This they do intentionally to get regular long-term income. Similarly, multinational companies (MNCs) use paid media and famous celebrities for advertisements and sell its useless junk food, cold drinks, and other products to spoil your health.

For body health, a person should follow three simple rules:

1. To have **simple food habits**. A person should keep in mind the calorie intake in proportion to physical work.
2. To **give up bad habits** such as smoking, alcohol, eating junk food, excessive eating, and the like.

3. To have some sort of discipline for a **physical workout**. Yoga is the best option, but there are other alternatives too—brisk walk and other simple physical exercises that keep your internal organs healthy and active."

5

MIND HEALTH

Religious preachers, personality motivators, psychiatrists, and also some fake religious *gurus* take advantage of a confused state of mind. We become their blind followers, and finally end up wasting our time, energy, and money. To lead a peaceful and stress-free life, we need to follow three main principles.

1. **Avoid jealousy**, anger, hatred, selfishness, gossip, comparison with others, and criticism in our approach to life. These are

the root causes of at least 50 per cent of stress.

2. We should have a clear career vision for livelihood and also develop a hobby for occupying us during our free time. Then we should try to achieve these by believing in the **"best efforts theory."** Always remember that the only difference between an ordinary person and an extraordinary person is the word "extra," which means extra sincere efforts, hard work, and practice.

3. To **believe in humanism**, brotherhood, empathy, and to live in harmony with Mother Earth.

Happiness can be achieved in two ways: contentment (spiritual way) and fulfilment of desires (materialistic route by following the "deserve then reserve" principle).

The thumb rule is to live a self-driven, contented life rather than a market-driven or consumerism lifestyle propagated by MNCs through paid media, brainwashing our mind by featuring celebrities in their advertisements or commercials.

We all have enormous power and peace within us, but we are ignorant of this. This is similar to a musk deer that has a source of fragrance in its belly but searches here and there in the forest for it.

6

FINANCIAL HEALTH

The greed in human beings for wealth is limitless, which ends up in accumulation instead of its enjoyment. To live a financially secured life, we need to follow three golden rules.

1. **Financial literacy:** We should develop an understanding of basic concepts such as need, wants, luxury, and addiction, to get financial freedom.

a. **Need** means to arrange basic things for survival such as food, shelter, clothes, education, healthcare, and so on.

b. **Wants** cater to your comforts, convenience, hobbies, and entertainment, fulfilment of which leads to an easy, comfortable, relaxed, stress-free, and happy life.

c. **Luxury items** mean branded expensive products. These are purchased to show off wealth and to maintain high status among friends, colleagues, and the business community.

d. **Addiction** means a product that controls our body, mind, and soul; we become the slave of the product; examples are cigarettes, tobacco, alcohol, drugs, greed for money, and so on.

2. **Savings:** Each individual must save at least 30 per cent of income for difficult days. In case your income and expenses do not allow you to save the required amount, then instead of blaming others you should increase your qualifications and develop skills, and capabilities to increase your earning capacity.

3. **Financial freedom:** Our savings must be invested in income-generating assets. This is to have a passive regular income. This could help in planning retirement or becoming a financially self-sufficient and self-reliant person.

7

SECRETS AND POWERS
OF THE BODY

During my research and interaction with Himalayan yogis, I learned the concept of seven sacred chakras, or wheels, of the body. These are mentioned in tantric and yogic traditions of Hinduism. The word "chakra" is derived from the Sanskrit word for *wheel*. Indian yogis believe that these chakras exist in the body of living beings. They are coils of energy, or rotating whirlpools surrounding the spine. They are considered focal points for the reception and transmission of energies.

1. In all, there are **seven chakras in the body**: (i) the crown chakra, located at the top of the head; (ii) the third-eye chakra, at the centre of the forehead; (iii) the throat chakra; (iv) the heart chakra; (v) the solar chakra, near the belly button; (vi) the spleen chakra, near the lower abdomen; and (vii) the root chakra, located at the base of spine.

2. Similar to these seven chakras, classical music has **seven notes of melody**: Sa, Re, Ga, Ma, Pa, Dha, and Ni, which roughly correspond to the western Do, Re, Mi, Fa, Sol, La, and Ti. The ancient Vedic belief is that the seven notes correspond to each of the seven chakras within us. The chakra is

activated when the frequency of the note matches the frequency of the given chakra. "Om" (ॐ) is the single word that takes all seven notes into account. Hence, Om is an integral part of yoga and meditation.

3. There are **seven colours** (known as **VIBGYOR**: Violet, Indigo, Blue, Green, Yellow, Orange, and Red). These are combined to form one universal light or white light. These seven colours convert to white light, similar to seven frequencies of melody, combine to create a universal sound, Om.

4. Modern scientists also believe that there are **seven broad forms of energy**: mechanical, heat, chemical, radiant, electrical, sound, and nuclear. Ancient seers not only knew that each of these could be broken into seven constituent elements but also discovered a

way to combine multiple sources of energy into a single one. The meditation that they practiced on the banks of the rivers or inside the caves of the Himalayas was actually used to combine multiple energy forms into one. Through spiritual powers, ancient yogis were able to lift their bodies into the air. This they were able to do by altering the flow of electric currents into a magnetic field.

With the knowledge of seven chakras of our body, seven frequencies of melody combine to give the universal sound Om (ॐ), seven colours (VIBGYOR) to form one universal white light, and seven broad energies converted to one energy form; ancient sages were able to bring mind and body to still position—the *samadhi* stage—to activate their spiritual powers.

8

SECRETS AND POWERS
OF THE MIND

As per popular philosophies, there are four main mind control or meditation techniques; (i) mindfulness/disciplining of the mind, (ii) knowledge, (iii) prayer (iv) karma or welfare meditation.

The main objective behind mind control is "controlling wild thoughts using intellect and reasoning power."

(A) Mind:

The mind is like a wild horse. The more addictions and bad habits you have, the wilder is your mind. In twenty-four hours, roughly sixty thousand thoughts come to a person's mind. Through a disciplined lifestyle, virtues, and by using reasoning power, we can control these. Intellect is the whip that controls these wild thoughts.

The ancient sages were able to reduce wild thoughts from sixty thousand to zero. During the *samadhi* stage, when the mind thoughts become zero, the powers of the soul are awakened. During this stage, ancient sages used the power of the soul to travel the universe through the wormhole. They discovered the miracles of outer space, planets, astrology, stars, and galaxies that even in today's modern world scientists have not been able to achieve this.

(B) Meditation:

Meditation is the process of extracting toxic elements from the mind. Meditation provides us with nourishment for the soul; this is similar to food being offered to the body.

*The **metaphor of radio transmission** will give a greater understanding of the meditation process. Broadcasts from a radio station are transmitted invisibly in all directions. But only if the receiver is adjusted to that particular frequency, you catch or receive those broadcasts. Similarly, during meditation,*

when the mind is attuned to the supreme soul,
we are able to glimpse a part of it.

There are five stages of meditation:

1. The first stage is **relaxation**. Stray and wild thoughts always distract the mind. At this stage, we try to train the mind. This is to help the body to relax by keeping the wild thoughts aside. This stage needs constant practice.

2. The second stage is **contemplation**. In this stage, we observe, review, or examine the virtues of the soul. It is upgrading our *sanskars* and values leading to a positive flow of energy removing wild thoughts.

3. The third stage is **concentration**. Here we find the real taste of silence. The mind slows down. The number of thoughts flitting through it gets highly reduced. At this stage we develop virtues such as patience, tolerance, humility, clarity, determination, and enthusiasm, to reach the astral level.

4. The fourth stage is the **realisation of truth**. We start experiencing the sweetness of silent communion with the supreme soul. The mind gets filled up with peace, purity, love, wisdom, and power.

5. The final stage of meditation is **transformation**. At this self-actualisation and self-realisation

stage, we experience wisdom, peace, compassion, empathy, and contentment.

(C) Karma Philosophy:

Karma philosophy teaches us that we are the creators of our own little world. Karma philosophy has two basic principles.

1. "**What goes around comes around**," or the "law of cause and effect," or the "law of action and reaction," which means that if we *throw a ball at a wall, it rebounds to us.*

2. Karma is a **flow of energy in three forms**: thoughts, words, and action. This means that we need to keep our circle positive by having positive thoughts,

uttering positive words, and by doing good deeds or actions.

a. The first element of karma is **thoughts**. Thoughts are seeds of our actions. Many of our problems are a result of our unhealthy thinking and negative attitude towards self, life, and other people. Hence, think before you speak. To ensure that we have a positive karma cycle, the foremost step is to have positive thoughts.

b. The second element of karma is **words**. Those who say they know everything actually do not know anything. The fact is that those who know do not speak. If we cannot speak about something then it is better to be silent. If a person speaks or acts evilly, sorrow will surely follow him, similar to the cart moving behind the ox.

c. The third element of karma is **action**. Newton's first law is, "Every action has an equal and opposite reaction." Our life is indeed governed by the law of karma or the law of cause and effect or action and reaction. The field of karma is the place where people sow the seeds of actions; they reap the fruits in this life or the next life.

9

LOVE VERSUS LUST

Guruji told us that in today's materialistic world many people are involved in lustful activities that spoil personal, family and professional life. There is a great need to understand love in its true spirit to enjoy it in harmony with nature.

1. The first stage in love is **attraction**. This is similar to seeing a rose flower in the garden and liking it. It is natural and is a gift of nature. This can be due to biological or hormonal changes (generation of

testosterone and oestrogen in the body) during teenage or youth.

2. The second stage is **breaking the rose flower** from the bush. We may feel happy that we have a rose flower for that particular moment, but actually it's temporary and not lasting. This is similar to getting physical, by way of kissing or intimacy. But slowly love will lose its shine or freshness, like a withered rose flower.

3. The third stage is when **you bring a flower pot home**, to take care and nurture it. You can daily see the flower. This means living a happy married life socially, traditionally, and culturally acceptable to all in a civilised society. For this step, both partners need to have a stable career.

4. On the other hand, **lust is a psychological force** against nature and norms of the

civilised society. This is similar to forcefully plucking a flower from the garden in spite of clear instructions not to do that. You get yourself involved in lustful activities against all moral values expected from a civilised person. Lust produces an intense want for an object. It can create extreme emotions to fulfil desires and can make you wild. It can lead you to cross any limits without taking care of values and ethics. Lust can represent any form such as sexuality, money, or power. That is why, after greed and addiction, one of the main reasons for crime in the world is lust.

10

POWERS OF THE SOUL

There are three basic faculties of the soul—mind, intellect, and *sanskars* or subconscious mind.

1. **The mind** is a screen or field; thoughts, sensations, tastes, textures, images, ideas, and senses are projected on this. The brain is the control centre for the various processes of the body and mind. The mind has tremendous energy, which is active even in dreams. Bodily enjoyment, lust,

greed, and addiction misguide our mind to generate wild thoughts.

2. **Intellect** is a screening, filtering, and monitoring process. It generates reasoning, logical, understanding, decision-making, and judgment powers. It plays a major role in bringing positive and productive thoughts. It tames the wild thoughts and removes negative thoughts. Intellect is a subtle nonphysical entity; it belongs to the soul and is not part of the body. Intellect gives us permanent happiness, contentment, and blissfulness.

3. **Subconscious mind or *sanskars*** represents values, virtues, morals, personality traits, good habits, beliefs, tendencies, talent, instincts, and memories. Subconscious or *sanskars* are imprints on our soul that form the basis of our personality. *Sanskars* hold

archives of all previous as well as this birth's recorded experiences and actions.

■ ■ ■

The soul has mainly three functions:
1. To give and maintain life;
2. To express and experience its own unique life;
3. To get the punishment or rewards or fruits of actions performed in this and previous existences.

■ ■ ■

There are eight main powers of the soul:

1. **Power to withdraw:** The main principle is, "I don't want to react immediately. I want

to act or react after applying my intellect, reasoning power, and *sanskars*." This means returning to a state of inner peace—at any time, under any circumstances—which is the real nature of the soul.

2. **Power to pack up:** This means travelling with less baggage or travelling light, whether physical or mental. Never carry the baggage of past into your present and future. Never carry negative and waste thoughts with you. We should have a "move on" approach in life. Believe that the past is history, the future is mystery, and the present is a gift.

3. **Power to tolerate:** This means having a broad and open mind approach. It is a willingness to recognise and respect differences in opinions or beliefs; to respect others' perspectives and lifestyles.

4. **Power to accommodate:** Accept, adjust, and adapt to avoid any conflicts in any relationship. It means having a heart so big and generous that I am able to rise above all differences of character and personality, the way the ocean absorbs the rivers.

5. **Power to face:** Face unpleasant, challenging, and threatening situations with courage and wisdom.

6. **Power of discrimination:** Never be swayed by other people's demands, desires and opinions. Always avoid illusory ways of thinking arising out of negativity, superstition, and ignorance. Always follow the principles of natural justice by hearing both sides as a judge does.

7. **Power to decide and judge:** This means taking an unbiased decision without any prejudice.

8. **Power to cooperate:** Be a team member to make this earth a better place to live in. We should avoid jealousy and ego as it kills cooperation.

11

THE MYSTERIES OF THE SOUL
AND SPIRITUALITY

Learners from different countries present at the Himalayan ashram asked the Himalayan yogi questions about the soul and spirituality; a few of these are:

1. What is the purpose of the human body's presence on earth? Is it just a biological vessel with a reproductive system, or does it have a spiritual relationship with various philosophies and religions?

2. By using our body as a medium, what is the ultimate purpose of the soul while on earth?

3. How and through what source does the soul enter into a baby while it is in the mother's womb at the embryonic stage?

4. As per the Bhagavad Gita, the soul is considered eternal, immortal, and everlasting and can never be destroyed. If the same soul is eternal and is born and reborn multiple times, why has the current population of the world increased to around 7.2 billion? How does biological reproduction affect the multiplicity of the soul?

5. We have read and heard that ghosts or devils or wicked souls can enter into another person's soul and control that person completely. How does this happen?

6. After liberation—or enlightenment—of the soul, what does life beyond the union of the soul and the supreme soul constitute?

7. What about the concept of hell or heaven, as propagated by nearly all religions? Is there really a hell for bad souls and a heaven for good souls?

8. What is reincarnation? Why do only a few people remember their past lives?

9. How did the supreme soul originate? Who was the creator or source of the supreme soul? How were the main gods born? Who were the mother and father of these gods?

10. In many religions and philosophies, it is believed that God is present everywhere in this universe, even inside human beings, in the form of a soul. Without God's will, nothing can move or happen on earth. If

God is inside human beings and present everywhere, why and how do crimes such as murder, rape, corruption, and kidnapping— as well as natural disasters—occur?

■ ■ ■

The Himalayan yogi replied, "These are fascinating questions full of curiosity and creativity. Please note that there are many philosophies and theories for the existence of God, the soul, and the supreme soul. One of the arguments is that gods are aliens with higher bodily, intellectual, soul, and spiritual powers than those possessed by human beings. There is a high possibility that these aliens may be living on a different planet, in a different galaxy, solar system, or universe. It is assumed that there are many galaxies and more than fifty thousand planets similar to earth.

As per myth and some research, normal human beings can use up to 10 per cent of their brain, intellect, reasoning power, and soul capacity to control their body and conscious and subconscious mind. It is assumed that aliens or so-called gods living on other planets can use up to 80 per cent of their brain, intellect, and soul powers. They have greater supernatural and spiritual powers built into their body and soul. They have unlimited powers such as appearing at a different place within a few seconds, astral projection, telepathy, and knowing how to use a wormhole to travel from one planet to another. Modern human beings use external modern technological devices such as mobile phones, television, computers, aeroplanes, rockets, and satellites to approximate these powers."

Himalayan yogi said, "There is a possibility that aliens have come to earth from time to time in the past." The Himalayan yogi laughed and continued, "Maybe now they are not coming because of pollution on earth. These aliens might have shown their superpowers to ordinary human beings, which are possible through yoga, meditation, and spirituality. Instead of developing such supreme powers within themselves, normal people perceived these powers to be extraordinary and started worshipping the aliens as gods."

He then said, "Inner spiritual enlightenment is a long-lasting process. You get it by developing virtue and a positive attitude. To achieve this, as a first step, I request all of you to focus on extracting toxic elements from your body, mind, and soul. Spiritual inclination improves our personality when we imbibe attributes like discipline, virtue, patience, humility, and kindness—all of which help us achieve the material goals of life."

The yogi went on to say, "Answers to the above queries are based on my personal experience and knowledge. It is better for you to personally experience the powers of the body, mind, and soul. As you progress in your yoga, meditation, and spiritual learning, you will surely find answers to some of your queries."

12

TRAILER TO SHOW POWERS
OF THE BODY AND MIND

The ashram guruji said, "Today, before we end our self-reform course, I will prove to you the power of yoga and meditation. This process is known as vibrant yoga. It is named as such because during this process the body vibrates and rejuvenates due to the activation of all seven chakras. Please remember to correctly chant Om—which we already learned during our yoga and meditation sessions. You need to chant *A* using your belly; for chanting *U* use your diaphragm or chest, and chant *M* using your throat. The final loud sound of the combined AUM or Om (ॐ) should come from the mouth, and your breath should come out of both nasal passages."

We all sat in the peace hall in the Ashram. After doing initial yoga postures for ten minutes, which we had been practicing for the last few days, we meditated for five minutes. Then guruji started chanting Om and we all followed him, correctly chanting Om the way it was taught by him earlier. We kept our spine straight, at a ninety-degree angle to the floor, with our head and neck in an upward position.

I want to share my vibrant personal yoga and meditation experience with you. I am sure all the other learners in our group would have had similar experiences. My body, mind, and intellect came into combined energy with the seven chakras after around two minutes of continuously chanting Om.

My body started vibrating and rejuvenating. It was like experiencing an earthquake—but within my body. My spine, neck, and head were straight; the whole body started vibrating at full force. My eyes were closed. I felt a light shining at the centre of my forehead, the place known as the home of the third eye. I was breathing in from the left nostril and breathing out through the right nostril.

This body-vibration process continued for almost five minutes. I was sweating; it felt as if all the toxic elements were coming out in the form of sweat. I felt that my internal organs were in vibration. My heartbeat was fast. My blood pressure was moderate. My mind was almost thoughtless. I was not able to think of any sad or happy moments in that particular situation.

I was enjoying this body-vibration process—a blend of various mechanical, heat, chemical, radiant, electrical, sound, and nuclear energies.

These were activated through the seven chakras and the Om.

Without any extra effort from me, it was like I was dancing in a sitting position, kind of as if I were on autopilot dance mode. There was complete silence in the peace hall. Only a little bit of sound could be heard, which might have been because of the vibration of all the learners' bodies.

Suddenly, I heard the sound of the Om from guruji's mouth. Guruji said, "Now, I am deactivating this vibrant yoga and meditation. Initially, I will chant Om loudly, and then slowly you will all please decrease the Om sound. Please don't open your eyes till I instruct you to open them. It may be possible that at the last stage of this vibrant yoga and meditation, some of you might not have full strength and may start crying or laughing, but don't worry: it is normal. You can continue to cry or laugh as long as you want. This is considered an indication that your bad memories or unfortunate incidents as toxic elements have been extracted from your mind and intellect as a sign of completion of the vibrant yoga and meditation."

Guruji started chanting Om; we all did the same thing. Slowly the body stabilised. Body vibration slowed and then suddenly stopped. The moment the vibration in our bodies ended, crying and laughing could be heard. We opened our eyes. I don't know why, but I started laughing. I could see some of my batch mates laughing; others were crying.

This process lasted five minutes, and suddenly we stopped crying or laughing, but our bodies were still sweating. Once this process was over, we all looked at each other and smiled—smiles of happiness and satisfaction and relief from toxic elements. It was a kind of enlightenment for us, as that day we were actually able to feel and understand the powers of the body and mind.

Everybody began sharing their experiences with each other as to what they had felt during the vibrant yoga. Our experiences were unique and exceptional. I was not able to note down the experiences of each and every one, as they were too personal, but all shared that they felt relieved of the many tensions of their previous days. The main thing was that on that day they were delighted to know the powers and mysteries of the body and mind through vibrant yoga and meditation, which was considered the first stage towards spirituality.

■ ■ ■

Guruji said, "This was just a trailer or preview of what powers our body and mind have. In the first self-reform course itself, we cannot learn everything. As you are aware, human beings can only use around 10 per cent of their intellect and bodily power. Today during vibrant yoga and meditation, you all have used around 20 per cent of your body and mind power. Now you can imagine what will happen to your body and mind if you use them more and more. For many years, the body and mind have been behaving in a particular manner, so we need to awaken them in a phased manner; our nerves and organs will burst if we try to use the full power of the body and mind in the first attempt. That is why it is always recommended to do it under the guidance of an experienced mentor. Now you can continuously practice this while you are in the real world to increase the power of the body and the mind."

"By eating natural and organic food, you can regularly cleanse your body. This type of food is suitable for your bodies as per *ayurvedic*, naturopathic, and herbal philosophies. To live a stress-free peaceful spiritual life, you need to purify your soul by practicing virtues such as a positive attitude, empathy, reasoning, and welfare meditation. Also, you need to remove vices such as greed, lust, addiction, hatred, gossip, anger, and jealousy."

"To experience a higher level of meditation and spirituality, it is essential to cleanse your pineal gland, which is considered the resting place of the soul, or the third eye. We will explore and learn more about the mysteries of the body, intellect, and soul in the 'soul-awakening' course. The important thing is that in life you try to become a good human being. This you can do by purifying your soul and serving deprived persons through welfare meditation. Apart from self-reform, you need to involve yourself in social, legal, media, political, institutional, and religious reforms through welfare meditation. You'll then make a difference in the lives of deprived people, and make this world a better place."

13

INVESTMENT IN SMART VILLAGE DEVELOPMENT PROJECTS

Guruji told us, "One of the main objectives of meditation is to purify one's soul so that one can become a good human being.

There are four types of meditation. The first three are (1) mindfulness/control over mind, (2) prayer, and (3) knowledge; they are centred around self-reform whereas the fourth and the last meditation, that is, welfare meditation, is linked with reforming other people's lives to make this world a peaceful place to live in."

Guruji said, "People who come here to the ashram are under the impression that peace is attained once they purify their body and soul in a two-week yoga and meditation course. They forget that peace is also required in their surroundings and environment. Once you leave the ashram and rejoin your routine machine like materialistic life for livelihood, the question is, will you be able to continue this purification process or not? So we should plan something for the welfare of the society using welfare meditation."

Basically, what guruji conveyed to all learners of different countries is that instead of limiting our self-reform activities at the individual level, we should come forward to broaden its scope by helping the deprived people in the society through various reforms. Thus, it can become a win-win proposition for both society and us. All of us are aware of the flaws and corruption in the existing system in our respective countries and blame politicians, bureaucrats, and businessmen but never try to improve it ourselves.

In layman's language, self-reform is like cleaning our own house internally and externally. But if our neighbours do not clean their houses properly and regularly, then the locality you are living cannot be considered as clean. So, both self-reform and other reforms (social, legal, political, economic, religious, and so on) should be done simultaneously to clean the present corrupt system. This can be done by approaching the country's top institutional bodies as judiciary or top court of the country for help and, at the same time, awakening and empowering common citizens through various reforms, encouraging them to clean their surroundings and overall environment in a sustainable manner. Thus, it is both an individual and collective effort, and is important to make this world a better place to live in.

For better understanding, let's take the example of India. The public has deep-rooted prejudices in their minds based on caste, creed, and religion. The politicians are exploiting these prejudiced minds through divisive politics. These prejudiced and empty-stomach voters are easily lured and manipulated by corrupt politicians through freebies schemes, subsidies, reservations, unrealistic election manifestoes, and false promises during elections, which are nothing less than cheating, scamming, and defrauding the innocent deprived public. The situation is almost the same in other countries, whether underdeveloped, developing, or developed, with some changes, but bitter fact is that for centuries, the public has been exploited by rulers, politicians, bureaucrats, and businesspersons for control over natural resources (which are meant for citizens in equal proportion) and political power.

■ ■ ■

Guruji said, "People never understand why they accumulate permanent assets more than their requirement while they are living temporarily on this earth. There are billionaires like Bill Gates and Warren Buffett who want to do something to eradicate poverty and the evil practices prevalent in the society. The need is to motivate these types of rich people to invest in smart village development projects. This will bring prosperity at the root level of the economy and thus eradicate poverty, hunger, illiteracy and superstition and at the same time give some return on their investment.

There is a need to invest in smart village development projects instead of smart city projects. This is the time to avoid investment in speculative stocks, gold, and multiple houses, which lead to concentration and accumulation of wealth in few hands and deprive millions of people of their basic needs.

Regarding growth potential, there are 2.5 million villages in the world; in India, around 641,000. Almost 70 per cent of India's population still lives in rural areas. If we assume that 50 per cent of these villages are still not developed, then there is huge growth and investment potential for both farmers and investors.

Food is the only product for which demand will always remain till the human race exists. If our farmers are prosperous, they will be alert, aware, and awakened about their natural, civil, and legal rights, resulting in an enlightened society. This will challenge the corrupt political and economic system, and will make a clean political and democratic system as per the constitution of respective countries."

■ ■ ■

Under the guidance of guruji, ashram volunteers did a survey of a nearby village to initiate a smart village development project. This survey revealed the fact that the average income level of farmers was only around Rs. 30,000 per year. The living standard was poor. They did not have access to clean water for drinking and sufficient water for irrigation. Many farmers did not have toilets in their homes. Electricity was available only for four to five hours in the day. The villages had no proper connectivity through roads. There was no dispensary or hospital within a fifty-kilometre range. Most of the teachers were incompetent to teach, particularly those who had paid bribes to corrupt politicians to get the job. Migration in these villages was at a peak. Because of this, many villages had become ghost villages. On the other hand, during the survey, village women were found to be very cooperative, hardworking, aware, and focused but most of the men were alcoholic.

As per research, organic, natural, and herbal plants grown in hilly areas have medicinal and herbal properties. This is not only because of pure, clean air and better soil properties but also due to water coming from the roots of traditional trees and herbal plants. This herbal water is used to grow crops, vegetables, and fruits. Seeds are preserved in a very ritual and conventional way, that is, they are kept in containers made of dried agricultural products. It is practically pollution and pesticide-free natural farming and has the twin benefits of providing food and medicines curing many diseases. As part of welfare meditation to benefit society, learners and ashram volunteers planned to come forward to educate the consumers about all these medicinal features.

■ ■ ■

If investors directly invest in the primary sectors such as agricultural and dairy farming through smart village development projects, then a high level of growth can be brought about in the manufacturing and service sectors as well. This will generate employment in cities too. Thus, the route to make smart cities is through smart village development projects.

Ashram volunteers worked in smart village projects covering the following five main areas:

1. Increasing farmers' income levels by removing middlemen.

2. Upgrading children's education, developing their interest in extracurricular and sports activities.

3. Preserving of natural resources by planting more trees, rainwater harvesting, and so on. Volunteers and villagers even sowed seeds of cucumber, watermelon, and other easily grown fruits and vegetables in nearby forests, to keep the wild animals and monkeys from coming to the villages in search of food.

4. Initiating infrastructure development projects such as road, pavement, toilets, dispensaries, hospital, school, function hall for cultural activities at the village level.

5. Inculcating awareness among villagers about values, morals, and humanity as part of the self-reform process to free them from old prejudices. To alert and awaken them about their natural, civil, and legal rights and their duties and responsibilities so that during the election time they can elect the right candidate.

Investors who were willing to invest in such smart village projects were happy mainly for two reasons:

1. Investment opportunity at the root level of the economy through smart village projects, thus scalability scope in these projects for the long term as food is an essential item for our survival.

2. Fulfilling the social obligation through welfare meditation by improving the lives

of farmers and their children. This is done by investment at the root level of the economy, and protecting the environment for the next generation.

■ ■ ■

Farmers' Welfare and Cooperative Societies were formed in villages to do farming on a collective basis. Investors were approached instead of banks. Banks were avoided as these are considered fair-weather friends and only lend funds to projects of politically connected corporate houses, which become Nonperforming Assets (NPAs) or bad loans at a later stage for obvious reasons. Ashram volunteers were in constant touch with investment companies, venture capitalists, hedge funds, asset management companies, and high net worth investors. These investors got impressed with the smart village projects providing both investment and philanthropy opportunities.

■ ■ ■

Ashram volunteers realised that there will be huge growth potential in rural areas particularly after the success of smart village projects, which will increase the income level and purchasing power of farmers. Global real estate market for residential and commercial property is down. We can develop basic infrastructure by constructing low-budget houses, pavements, roads, clubs, schools, hospitals, dispensaries, toilets, rainwater harvesting system, solar, hydel and wind energy plants, warehouses, cold storage, marketplace, shops malls, and so on. Investors can directly invest in this smart village and community development projects instead of routine traditional and personal investments in multiple houses, speculative stock markets, precious metals, and stones, which only lead to the accumulation of wealth in few hands without any productive results.

■ ■ ■

Employees of corporate houses and students from various management schools, colleges, and universities can send their students to learn in the actual field rather than in classroom settings. Students can be motivated to join National Social Services (NSS), and they can visit villages for fifteen days every six months. If we wish to lessen the population burden on cities, we need to stop migration by creating employment and business opportunities at the village level through smart village projects. This is also important for the protection of the environment. More development at the village level means less pollution in cities.

■ ■ ■

To conclude Guruji said, "As all of you aware, our stay on this earth is temporary, and yet day and night we are busy in accumulating assets either on the pretext of financial security or for our kids. Most of the investors invest in fixed deposits, real estate, stock markets, and precious metals such as gold, diamond, and the like, without any productive results for them as well as for the common persons. This also leads to concentration of wealth in a few hands, with the majority of people suffering from lack of livelihood, essential amenities, and basic infrastructure. It is known that neither banks nor the government (which are controlled and manipulated by corrupt politicians and greedy businessmen) help farmers, and they become victims of middlemen and local money lenders forcing them to do suicides. If investors directly invest in the agricultural sector, then not only will farmers get the benefit (it will generate income for them and will prevent the suicide of farmers), but these investors too can get long-term extra income by investing in productive growth areas."

14

DON'T HATE POLITICS; HATE CORRUPT POLITICIANS

Some ashram volunteers consulted guruji to form a political party to contest elections to bring honest persons into politics. But guruji declined, saying, "Nowadays politics has become dirty, and we need to avoid indulging in this dirty game."

I said, "Guruji, you always say that politics is another form of social service. The only difference between social service and politics is that politicians have access to taxpayers' money and they can also borrow international funds for public welfare, but social workers always lack funds. Instead of using public funds for public welfare, corrupt politicians convert these funds for their personal benefit. If we help honest people to reach the state legislative assembly or parliament through fair politics, we can stop misuse of public funds. We can also have control over natural resources, which corrupt politicians and businesspersons are exploiting for their greed."

Finally, guruji gave permission to form and register a political party in the name of Human Welfare Party. He put some conditions—the political party should not have any link with ashram, ashram learners will only work as volunteers, they will not contest elections; election campaigning will be solely based on merits; there should be a positive election campaign without getting involved in any controversy; candidates would be selected based on their profile, past experience, character, and reputation; there should not be any criminal charges or cases pending against any candidate; money would be spent to a bare minimum; and core issues relating to farmers and poor people would be highlighted during the election campaign.

Guruji advised us that the principles of Bhagavad Gita (karma philosophy and welfare meditation); Chanakya-Chandragupta's economic and political teachings; and modern business, marketing, administration, and management strategies could be adopted and adapted to manage this newly formed political party.

Guruji specifically focused on the ambitiousness of candidates and party workers, as this is one of the main reasons for the failure and break up of many political parties.

Five teams were formed:

1. **Chanakya team (kingmakers or strategists or intellectuals):** This team com-prised of retired judges, army personnel, professors, principals, teachers, doctors, lawyers, bankers, financial consultants, engineering graduates, architects, authors, celebrities, sportspersons, business and management professionals, and so on. These persons should not have any ambition and interest in holding political posts for the initial five years. Their role as strategists would be crucial in guiding and enlightening the aspiring leaders to reform the society. The mantra of Chanakya team should be **"Don't hate politics, hate corrupt politicians."**

2. **Chandragupta team** (aspiring politicians or leaders who can hold portfolios as ministers). Persons who are already leaders in their professional or business life such as managing directors, chief executive officers (CEOs) of big corporates, social workers, activists, teachers, retired army officers, ex-captains of sports teams, and the like. They should not be keen to enter politics for earning money but should want to serve the public. They should have a clean image and want to serve the public through welfare meditation.

3. **Financial supporters or investors or businesspersons:** Those having neither time nor interest in becoming part of Chanakya team or Chandragupta team. They are willing to financially support

the new political party and smart village projects for twin benefits. First, for their long-term business sustainability, and second, to reform the society by helping farmers, poor people, and their children.

4. **Social reformers:** Those who have expertise in fields relating to public welfare, education, healthcare, tourism, organic and herbal farming, infrastructure development, construction, import-export, defence, and so on; who can make plans and policies to remove poverty and illiteracy from the country.

5. **Social workers or volunteers:** School and college students, ashram volunteers, activists, NGO workers, corporate employees, and so on. Apart from helping in the implementation of smart village

projects, they can work on a part-time basis by directly or indirectly interacting with voters. They can work under the supervision of the Chanakya, Chandragupta, and/or reformers team. Initially they can educate and convince voters about the importance of electing a deserving honest candidate to rule the state or the country. Later on they can keep an eye on the implementation of development projects.

■ ■ ■

Ashram volunteers prepared a list of independent candidates having a clean image. These candidates had lost elections in the past with marginal difference. They were willing to contest the election again. Before selection, the volunteers investigated their profile, character, reputation, experience, background, and source of income.

For election campaigns, big greedy corporate houses financially support the established national and regional parties; arranging funds for new political parties is always a big challenge.

■ ■ ■

The Chanakya team of the Human Welfare Party, after consulting the Indian Institute of Management (IIM) graduates, suggested contesting the elections professionally. They recommended applying modern concepts and methods for advertising, publicity, sales, marketing, business management and administration, and project implementation strategies to give the best value to voters for their votes.

Chanakya team suggested to follow the AIDA principles for advertisement and publicity—Awareness, Interest, Desire, and Action:

1. Publicity to spread **awareness** about candidates of Human Welfare Party associated with Farmers Welfare Society,

2. Publicity to arouse the **interest** of voters based on candidates' profile and clean image,

3. Creating a **desire** among voters to vote for honest candidates based on their credentials,

4. Voters finally taking **action** on the election day to cast a vote in favour of the party's candidates.

Chandragupta team suggested the following four Ps: Product, Place, Promotion, and Price factors of Sales and Marketing propounded by renowned international marketing guru Mr. Philip Kotler:

1. The **product**—a qualified and honest candidate with a clean image,
2. **Place**—a candidate who is well versed with the local area and its issues,
3. **Promotion**—to promote the candidate using AIDA principles of advertising and publicity,
4. **Price**—emphasising to the voters the need to elect an honest candidate instead of a wrong candidate. The wrong candidate can misuse public funds, something they had been doing for many years.

Chanakya team suggested keeping in mind Abraham Harold Maslow's motivational theory to select candidates. It recommended selecting candidates who are at the **self-actualisation stage** of their career and life and are willing to serve the public through welfare meditation route. Human Welfare Party should ensure that the primary motive of the candidates in joining politics is social service and not greed, ambitiousness for power, or to hide criminal activities under VIP security at the cost of taxpayers' money.

15

POLITICAL REFORMS

Guruji requested me to prepare a report on political, legal, media, institutional, and religious reforms required in the country, which he wanted to send to the top court judges for their review and consideration.

In a few days, I prepared a draft report on various reforms required to clean the existing corrupt system and submitted it to guruji for his review, inputs, and final evaluation. This report contained details to bring happiness in the lives of millions of people through reforms using welfare meditation.

Guruji said, "I will review this draft report. Meanwhile, I suggest you share this draft report on social media to seek comments from the general public. We need to effectively use the social media to make the general public aware, alert, and awakened. Reforms are required in each and every country of the world. Global citizens can customise these reforms as per their country's situation, conditions and requirements. We need to convince the country's top court judges that this is the common voice of citizens to initiate the reforms. We cannot rely any more on corrupt politicians and bureaucrats to bring reforms as so far they have miserably failed to take any concrete step to eradicate poverty, hunger, illiteracy, and superstition."

■ ■ ■

Political Reforms: Someone has correctly said, "Politics is the last resort for scoundrels," which fits very well the current corrupt political scenario. There are many black spots in the history of Indian democracy; politicians who had held portfolios of chief ministers or ministers in state or in central government for several years as lawmakers were, later on, declared lawbreakers or criminals or convicts by the top court. Ironically and unfortunately, these convicts made laws during their tenures as lawmakers and members of state legislative assembly and parliament. Is this not a mockery of Indian judiciary, democracy, and the constitution that criminals made the laws?

Actually, our constitution is great as it has provisions to make an ordinary person the president or the prime minister of the country till such time as criminal charges against that person are proven in any court of law, a process that takes years. This is because of an adversary or rivalry legal system manipulated by influential lawyers-cum-touts for their powerful clients having muscle, black money, and link powers at their disposal after holding constitutional positions such as ministers. These corrupt or criminal politicians misuse such flexible provisions or loopholes in the legal system and the constitution for their own benefit. Once they come to power, they not only avail VIP security but also misuse government investigation agencies and machinery; regulatory, statutory, and financial institutions; and autonomous constitutional bodies as caged parrots, attack dogs, lapdogs, and puppets to destroy all facts, evidence and witnesses against them. There is a need to have fast track courts for such accused politicians wherein support of the court's detective and investigative arm can be taken for effective and speedy trial in a time-bound manner.

There is a lokpal bill or ombudsman bill pending for final approval in many states and at central government level, but it is obvious and makes sense that corrupt politicians would not wish to pass such a law that is against them. Instead of depending on politicians, the top court should take suo moto action or initiative to form a special committee of retired judges to prepare a lokpal bill in a time-bound manner to curb the powers of corrupt politicians and bureaucrats. The top court and high courts need to send reminders to central or state governments every three months to pass the lokpal bill in the state legislative assembly or parliament, and, if not passed even after four reminders, it should be considered as contempt of court.

A committee comprising of retired judges from the top court and retired commissioners of the election commission should be formed to scrutinise political funding particularly from big corporates and foreign sources, and review all election manifestoes of the national and regional political parties that they have released since independence to fool innocent voters by making false and unrealistic promises. Politicians being the service providers to taxpayers and voters who have equal rights over the country's natural resources, should be held liable for providing defective service or for nondelivery of services to consumers within the purview of Consumer Protection Acts.

Accountability and responsibility should be fixed on the political party's president and prime minister for false and unrealistic promises made by their party workers, politicians, and ministers to cheat the innocent public to get their votes just to come to power.

In today's corrupt political atmosphere, the last hope is only from the top court to play a proactive role to uphold and protect the institutions in India keeping in mind the spirit of the preamble of the constitution—justice, liberty, equality, and fraternity—to ultimately protect the rights of citizens of India.

We should try our best and need to endeavour at the individual level to reform the political system. We can do this through collective efforts. Unfortunately, many intellectuals feel that present politics is dirty and that they should avoid dirtying their hands. The mantra should be—don't hate politics; rather we should hate the corrupt politicians. All intellectuals and retired persons particularly senior citizens should come forward to make aware, alert, and awaken the common citizens with regard to their electoral rights and obligations.

Thus investors, intellectuals, and retired persons have to play a very important role to clean the corrupt political system. Also when our farmers become prosperous through smart village development projects, they will be alert, aware, and awakened about their natural, civil, and legal rights, resulting in an enlightened society. This will challenge the corrupt political system and will make a clean political, economic, and democratic system as per the spirit of the constitution.

16

LEGAL REFORMS

The present judiciary is based on the adversary or rivalry legal system. In this system, there are chances that powerful parties having muscle and money power can twist facts, manipulate evidence, and buy or threaten witnesses to make their case strong against a weaker parties. They do this with the help of influential lawyers-cum-touts.

There is a need to promote and adopt an inquisitorial or investigative legal system wherein an investigative and detective arm is provided to judges at the lower, higher, and top court level to independently cross check and verify facts and evidence before they give a final judgement. This will also give threat to powerful parties and their influential lawyers-cum-touts that their facts, evidence, and witnesses can be investigated, re-examined, and cross-verified by judges through its independent investigative and detective arm before giving final judgements.

This investigative and detective arm will help in building the trust of the general public in the judicial system. It will also help in resolving millions of pending cases in a time-bound manner to protect legal, civil, and natural rights of common citizens for whom otherwise "justice delayed means justice denied."

Fee for such investigative and detective services can be taken as part of court fee, or as cess included in taxes and duties collected by the state or central government but must be kept under the control of the top court.

The scope of these detective and investigative arms of courts can be widened by giving them powers to coordinate with international investigative agencies, International Police (INTERPOL), relevant cybercrime teams, and agencies dealing in international money laundering activities. This is to check whether corrupt politicians, bureaucrats and greedy businessmen have diverted their undeclared and undisclosed income collected out of country's taxpayers' funds and from borrowed international funds; and they taken bribes from MNCs and drug and weapon dealers to their foreign bank accounts of shell companies in tax heaven countries.

The legal reforms suggested above are at institutional level and will take their time. We should always endeavour for these reforms through collective efforts.

At the individual level, we need to understand that life is short and, instead of taking a false ego position, we should have a "move-ahead approach" in life to live a peaceful and stress-free life. Friends come and go, but enemies always stay in our mind. Mediation is an alternate way to resolve disputes and, through mediation millions of pending legal disputes in courts relating to civil issues and marriage can be resolved amicably not only between two individuals but also between two countries, with the aim to make this world a better and more peaceful place to live. Hence, we need to develop and practice the "move-ahead approach" to resolve our disputes amicably. This will help individuals to have time and energy for developing their skills and pursuing hobbies.

17

MEDIA REFORMS

There are a few international religious secret societies along with MNCs and drugs and arms dealers who have disrupted and disturbed world peace through corrupt politicians. In many countries such as Syria, Somalia, Iraq, Afghanistan, and so on there is poverty, unemployment, ignorance, superstition, and illiteracy. These people are labelled as fundamentalists through propaganda by puppet media. The actual fact is that they need food to survive. Powerful capitalist nations and weapon manufacturers create unrest in these countries for their greed and political powers. Then they sell their technologically outdated armaments to both the rulers and the rebels in these countries. This serves multiple purposes—terrorising the world by killing innocent people, disreputing the religions, selling their weapons, expanding their businesses, sourcing oil and raw materials at cheap rates, and selling finished products in underdeveloped and developing countries, to name a few. Modern investigative journalism can expose these hidden aspects and make aware, alert, and awaken the global public.

Media is not exposing the nexus of international terror forces patronised by capitalist countries and MNCs that are weakening the sovereignty of developing and underdeveloped countries by bribing politicians. Nowadays media is run as a business and has been restricted to accidents, corruption at lower levels, street fights, road rage incidents, eve-teasing cases, honour killings, mob lynching incidents, religion and caste-based violence, and useless, illogical debates on TV channels; media is just doing infotainment to increase Television Rating Points (TRP) for advertisement revenue.

What are journalists doing? They highlight social, economic, and political issues, but to whom? To the sufferer—the innocent general public—or to the creator of these nuances or issues—the corrupt politicians and bureaucrats, who will never resolve these issues for their ill motives? There are around five hundred news channels in India. What have they been doing for so many years? Whole day long they repeatedly highlight the same issue to the public for the sake of TRP and advertisements. They do this without any concrete solutions to improve the lives of the general public. The scope of journalism should be broadened. Instead of just highlighting issues, it should ensure a solution by constantly following up with the concerned authorities to resolve the issues. This is required to uphold the true spirit of democracy and the constitution. Soldiers are fighting at borders to protect the country from external terror forces. Similarly, journalists, as soldiers of media, need to fight with corrupt internal forces to protect the public.

Media is always considered the fourth pillar of democracy and the saviour of the constitution along with judiciary. It must question the establishment, but unfortunately it has become their propaganda machinery.

There is no doubt that the media run by corporate business houses instead of guiding is misguiding the general public. They are doing this for the sake of TRP to get advertisement. It is a known fact that the cost of advertisements that corporate houses run on the news channel is ultimately recovered from customers or audience in the form of higher product cost. This is over and above wasting their valuable time while watching the propaganda news and sponsored advertisements.

■ ■ ■

A **media cess**, kept under the control of the top court, can be collected from the public as happens in many Western countries. This is for making the media impartial and neutral from the clutches of corrupt politicians and businessmen. This way, media can keep an eye on the development works as per election manifestoes issued by ruling political parties.

■ ■ ■

Independent, impartial, **autonomous authority** under the supervision of the top court should be formed to oversee the functioning of these news channels. This impartial and independent authority should endeavour to make media the fourth pillar of democracy in its true sense. Independent and neutral Internet web-based news portals that run their channels by subscription and donation should be promoted and supported by the autonomous authority to encourage fair competition and honest reporting in the media industry.

■ ■ ■

Any institutional reform takes its own time. To hasten this media reform process, we need to spread awareness about the nexus between corrupt politicians and media companies through social media.

At the individual level, we need to understand that nowadays media is earning money by misguiding audience through propaganda and fake news. It is well known that television is considered as an idiot box, a time-consuming and money-reducing machine, as it affects the quality time required to spend with the family, or for a career, or hobby.

Media has become a propaganda tool for politicians to spread rumours. The simple step is to avoid watching news channels and focus on your career development, family, and hobbies— this will surely bring peace in your family life and in the world.

18

RELIGIOUS REFORMS THROUGH HUMANISM PHILOSOPHY

Guruji said, "The objective of self-reform is to become a good human being with a pure soul, by involving yourself in the service of others through welfare meditation."

Guruji further said, "Your parents are just **biological parents**. Their duty is to help you to settle down in your career. Your **real parents** are in the form of morals, discipline, humbleness, manners, empathy, and virtues, which make you a good human being and guide you throughout life.

Your **grandparents** are in the form of *sanskars*, values, culture, traditions, customs, and heritage to keep you connected to your roots. It seems because of greed, lust, and addiction we have forgotten all these teachings."

■ ■ ■

Religious reforms by spreading humanism philosophy: This world has diversity by religions, castes, languages, cultures, and heritages, which is similar to having different flowers in a garden. Unfortunately, through divisive politics, politicians have misused this unique feature. They rule by spreading hatred among the public using puppet media.

Almost all religions have failed in achieving the objective of inner peace and world peace. So, there is a great need to inculcate and promote humanism philosophy at the school level to make this world a peaceful, pollution free, and better place to live in.

Five main principles that should be covered in the **humanism philosophy** are:

1. Striving for self-reform and social reform through National Social Service (NSS), welfare meditation, and smart village projects.

2. Having respect and care for **Mother Earth** to protect the environment.

3. Being a **good human being** by having empathy, respect for the perspectives of others, developing a sense of brotherhood, and secularism.

4. Giving importance to **virtues, values and morals** in school and college curriculum.

5. **Avoiding vices** such as greed, lust, and addiction, as these are the leading causes of most of the crimes in the world.

Guruji said, "The root cause of today's social, financial, business, legal, media, environmental, religious, and political degradation is the lack of virtues, values, and morals. Desires are limitless, and we need to understand the basic difference between need, want, luxury, and addiction to live a stress-free life. The existing corrupt system can be cured through self, social, political, media, institutional, and legal reforms and by following righteous, virtuous and spiritual path."

After interacting with Himalayan yogis and learning about self-reform and welfare meditation at the ashram, our perspective towards life has changed. We learned how to use intellect and reasoning power to inculcate virtuous qualities such as empathy, positive attitude, social reform, and following the principle "deserve, then reserve" to develop skills and capabilities to aspire for material wealth.

We also learned how to distance ourselves away from vices such as greed, lust, and addiction to live a stress-free peaceful life.

GLOSSARY OF INDIAN TERMS FOR GLOBAL READERS

Ayurveda. One of the world's oldest holistic ("whole-body") healing systems.

Bhagavad Gita. An ancient Indian text, meaning the "Song of the Lord," about philosophy and spirituality.

Chakra. Sanskrit word used for "wheel."

Chanakya. An ancient Indian teacher, philosopher, economist, jurist, and royal advisor.

Chandragupta. The founder of the Maurya Empire in ancient India. Pupil of Chanakya or Kautilya.

Devbhoomi. Land of deities and gods and Uttarakhand in India is considered such a place.

Guru. A spiritual teacher, tutor, sage, counsellor, mentor, master.

Haridwar. A religious and spiritual place in Uttarakhand, India.

Karma. Good or bad luck, viewed as resulting from one's actions.

Om (ॐ). A mystic syllable, considered the most sacred mantra in Hinduism.

Rishikesh. A religious and spiritual place in Uttarakhand, India.

Samadhi. Bringing mind and body to a still position to activate spiritual powers.

Sanskars. Traditions, principles derived from cultural ethos.

Tantric. Enlightenment through mystical and magical processes.

Uttarakhand. A hilly state in India, located in the Himalayan range.

Vedic. Relating to the Veda or Vedas. The language of the Vedas, an early form of Sanskrit.

Yoga. A Hindu spiritual and ascetic discipline widely practised for health and relaxation.

Yogis. A person who is proficient in yoga.

ABOUT AUTHOR RAVI DABRAL'S
FORTHCOMING FICTION NOVEL:

GREED
LUST ADDICTION

(Victory over vices makes you champion)

Materialism versus Spiritualism-I

Materialism is the mantra of the modern generation, which regards "sensual pleasure" as the purpose of life. The motto is, **"Eat, drink and be merry,"** for once the body is reduced to dust or ashes there is no hope of coming back again on this Earth. This philosophy gives rise to ***greed, lust, and addiction***, which are ***vices*** within us.

As against materialism philosophy, ***spiritualism,*** which was the guiding principle of our ancient generations, and is still adopted by a limited few, believes in having ***virtues, values, and morals*** to live a contented, stress-free, and purposeful life to finally get enlightenment.

This is the journey of an investigative journalist, thrillingly revealing mysteries of the corrupt material world. Believing in following the virtuous, righteous and spiritual path in life, how far will he succeed in a society dominated by corrupt politicians, unscrupulous greedy businessmen, puppet media, insensitive police, and even a biased judiciary?

Will he survive in the midst of the powerful lobbies, who have scant regard for human life, when it comes in the way of their road to power and money? Or will he be crushed like a beetle under a booted foot, as everyone predicts? Or will he be able to stand up just with the help of a handful of yogis of the Himalayan ashrams and their spiritual followers?

A story with lots of twists, turns, conflicts, romance, emotions, drama, suspense, thrill and action, promising a mesmerising reading experience…

For further details about the author, please visit **www.ravidabral.com**.

For any feedback and suggestions, please e-mail at **info@ravidabral.com**.

To share your views as to how we can make this world a better and more peaceful place to live in through self-reform and other reforms mentioned in this book, please follow Ravi Dabral on social media at:

Facebook: https://www.facebook.com/ravi.
dabral.12

Twitter: www.twitter.com/dabralravi

YouTube: http://www.youtube.com/user/ravidabral

Instagram: http://instagram.com/ravi.dabral

LinkedIn: https://www.linkedin.com/in/
ravi-dabral-9b4711110/

ACKNOWLEDGEMENTS

Yogis of Himalayas, gurus of various ashrams in Uttarakhand, ashram volunteers, corporate and personal friends, and renowned personalities who shared their experiences and knowledge for the benefit of global readers and citizens to make this world a better, safer, and more peaceful place to live in.

ABOUT AUTHOR RAVI DABRAL

 Author Ravi Dabral is the winner of International Man of Excellence Award for Education, Corporate & Social Services.

Ravi has over twenty-five academic and professional qualifications.

He is a fellow member of seven international institutes active in the field of arbitration, mediation, corporate services, cost and management accountancy, ship broking, and so on.

Ravi was born in Uttarakhand, famous for spiritual ashrams and known as *"Devbhoomi,"* the abode of deities and gods. The influence of his early years in this land of spirituality can be seen in most of his works.

He has been a commodity trader for over two decades. He is based in Singapore, one of the best international trading hubs in the world.

Ravi has got diplomas in creative writing from Open Minds International, Singapore; script writing and direction from Film and Television Technology Institute (FTTI), India; and has done a course in creative writing, acting and dance from Anupam Kher's Actor Prepares.

Ravi's background from Uttarakhand, a famous spiritual place in India; multiple qualifications in economics, political science, laws, commerce, and so on; over two decades' experience as an international commodity trader; courses in creative writing; and keen interest in entrepreneurship, psychology, philosophy, and spirituality makes him a well-versed and fully equipped author to write nonfiction and fiction books in the domain of "materialism versus spiritualism," keeping in mind both the sensual and spiritual pleasure of the global readers, with learnings on how to live a healthy, wealthy, and happy life.

Ravi is associated with clean environment NGO (www.swachhparyavaran.com) as a consultant.

He has the vision to instil virtuous traits in students and the young generation to make this world a better and more peaceful place to live in.

Ravi is married to Sarita (a teacher) and has two children, Namita and Avi.

To know more about Ravi Dabral, please visit **www.ravidabral.com**.

For any feedback and suggestions, please e-mail at **info@ravidabral.com**.

CPSIA information can be obtained
at www.ICGtesting.com
Printed in the USA
LVHW092329100520
655330LV00005B/1619